Amazing Animal Adventures

# Around the World

with Brian Keating

# BRIAN KEATING'S AMAZING ANIMAL ADVENTURES

A Ton of Wrinkles

Kittiwakes

Arctic Ocean

Ellesmere Island (Canada): "A Ton of Wrinkles"

Canada

Norway: "Petrel Puke and Headless Kittiwakes"

Europe

North America

Atlantic Ocean

Pacific Ocean

Africa

Guyana: "Things That Fly By in the Night"

Equator

Ecuador

Ghana: "Saving Ghana's Hippos"

Galapagos Islands (Ecuador): "Looking into the Eyes of Godzilla"

South America

Saving Ghana's Hippos

The Eyes of Godzilla

Things That Fly By...

Southern Ocean

Antarctica: "The Penguin Superhighway"

N

0    1500    3000 km

Penguin Superhighway

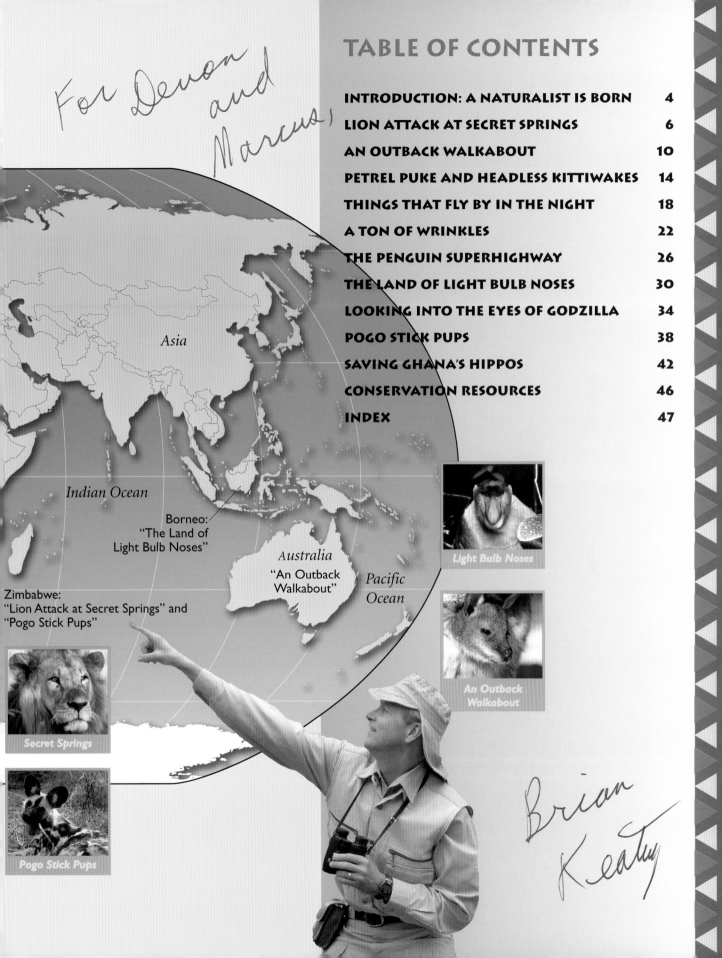

For Devon and Marcus,

# TABLE OF CONTENTS

Asia

Indian Ocean

Borneo:
"The Land of
Light Bulb Noses"

Australia
"An Outback
Walkabout"

Pacific
Ocean

Zimbabwe:
"Lion Attack at Secret Springs" and
"Pogo Stick Pups"

Light Bulb Noses

An Outback
Walkabout

Secret Springs

Pogo Stick Pups

Brian Keating

# A NATURALIST IS BORN

I was born in Medicine Hat, Alberta, but lived there for only the first 6 years of my life. My sister was born deaf and my parents wanted her to learn how to speak, so we moved to New York. In those days, the Lexington School for the Deaf in New York City was the only place that taught deaf kids how to speak.

When I was in grade seven and eight, I built a three-room underground fort, deep in the woods near where I grew up. I did some great birdwatching at the fort's hidden entrance.

So in a 1957 Chevy and a homemade trailer that looked like a silver teardrop, my parents drove with four kids under the age of eight to New York. I remember my father telling me the story of going the wrong way down a one-way street in Manhattan. He had just turned a corner and saw a wall of traffic coming toward us. He looked over and a guy was standing beside us on the curb. My dad said "What do I do?" and the guy looked at him, looked up and down the street, and said, "Pull a u-turn whydoncha?"

I developed my interest in birdwatching in New York, my home for 11 years. I'll never forget a day of discovery when I was 12 years old. We lived near 8 hectares (20 acres) of forestland, and I was walking in the rain on a trail in the woods. I was trying to stay dry under a garbage pail lid I'd found, and suddenly a scarlet tanager landed on the tree in front of me. It was only a few meters away, and through my binoculars I could see this beautiful bird perfectly. I remember gasping aloud at the sight and I was hooked. Birdwatching became a passion that later branched into all areas of natural history.

My parents encouraged my interest in nature and sent me to summer school courses on marine biology, archeology, and dinosaurs. I once found the skeleton of a dead rat under a barn we'd pulled down and I decided to put it back together. So I met with the curator at New York's Museum of Natural History, and he loaned me a book that included an exploded view of the skeletal system of the rat. I followed the diagram carefully and assembled my collection of tiny bones into a skeleton. I still have that skeleton in a box in my basement.

Our family moved back to Canada once my sister was able to attend a regular school. I went to Lakeland College in Vermilion, Alberta, and, later, to Brandon University in Manitoba, to study fish and wildlife, and I spent virtually all of my spare time climbing mountains, skiing, camping, and hiking. When I graduated, I landed a job as a naturalist in southern British Columbia and couldn't believe my good fortune. Here I was, being paid to learn more about nature!

I met Dee while we were both working with the Canadian Wildlife Service. We were new naturalists and felt a little stressed because we had to know so much and knew so little. So we teamed up and worked as partners to build our knowledge. We went on many birdwatching and plant identification missions together. Our working relationship slowly developed into a weekend hiking relationship, which eventually led to our marriage. We're still best friends to this day. I think we're both at our best when we're in wilderness environments.

When Dee was accepted at the University of Calgary to study medicine, I found out about a job at the Calgary Zoo and landed a position as the director of their education department. I had that job for 15 years. I now direct the Calgary Zoo's conservation outreach program, which allows me to help conservation projects around the world. This kind of outreach is what I believe a zoo's primary mission should be.

Zoos have a strong profile in the community and a lot of power to do good things. Already a great tool for education, a good zoo is also the perfect tool for important conservation work. What's more, zoos can play a big role in getting people interested in the natural world. If you talk to the world's famous biologists, many will tell you they had their first inspiration at a zoo. And more and more zoos are developing exciting positions like mine.

Last year the Calgary Zoo supported a dozen conservation projects around the world, including a park in Ghana to preserve one of the two remaining hippo populations in that country. You can read more about this park later in the book.

I hope you will see in these stories some of the amazing people, places, plants, and animals that have inspired me to learn more about nature and to seek the world's wild spaces. Maybe something in these stories will inspire you too.

**When the Calgary Zoo hosted Jane Goodall, the famous primate researcher, on her first visit to Calgary, Dee and I took her to the mountains for a Canadian wildlife experience.**

# LION ATTACK *at* SECRET SPRINGS

The scariest day of my life happened in a place I call Secret Springs, though that's not its real name. I've never identified the real place because I want to keep it a secret. The spring is a place in Zimbabwe where water trickles out of the ground about 60 kilometers (37 mi.) from the nearest river. Dee and I usually spend a week there each September, at the height of the dry season, with our friend Garth Thompson, who helps us organize group tours from his home in Africa.

The dry season in Africa has to be experienced to be believed. It's so hot and so dry I get thirsty just thinking about it. Everything seems to be craving water. So when I find a place like Secret Springs, it's the center of life. Being there is like being in a National Geographic film.

One year, we arrived at the spring in the middle of the day, when it was very hot and dry and there was hardly any wildlife moving. Garth walked on one side of the spring and we walked on the other to check for spoor. Spoor would tell us the number of buffalo coming to the spring and if there were any leopards, hyenas, or lions in the area.

When we met up again with Garth, he said that he had seen a pride of female lions heading off in the other direction. He'd also seen the male, sitting alone under a flat-top acacia tree.

There was a big ravine between us and the lion, so Garth suggested that we head over to

A male lion weighs about 189 kilograms (420 lb.) and is about 2.7 meters (9 ft.) long, measured from his nose to the tip of his tail.

The average lion pride consists of about thirteen cats, but prides can have up to forty members.

watch the lion through our binoculars for a while. The lion was a long way off—probably 75 meters (250 ft.) from the far edge of the ravine—so we weren't pushing his "fight or flight" distance. As long as the lion's females weren't around, and we weren't crowding him by getting too close, we felt perfectly safe.

So we walked toward the ravine in full view of the male, tremendously self-confident that what we were doing was perfectly fine. But just before we got there, I had a premonition. I suddenly wondered if we were making a mistake. I took one more step to the edge of the ravine and I was looking into the eyes of four female lions and two cubs. Immediately three females came at us in an attack. Growling and snarling, they catapulted out of the ravine in a burst of roaring feline fury, teeth bared, faces pulled back, muscles flexed. The fourth female and cubs disappeared down the ravine in a shot of dust.

Within seconds we were running backwards as fast as we could. We all knew that you should never turn your back on a charging lion, because if you do, the lion's predator-prey instinct kicks in. So we faced the lions and ran backwards yelling "Oi oi oi oi oi!" I couldn't believe how loud Dee was yelling. She's got vocal chords that I'd never heard before! I kept looking over my shoulder because the elephants had flattened most of the bushes in the area and there were stumps sticking up everywhere. I imagined my heel hitting one of them and falling flat, with a lion on top of me a second later.

## SAY THE WORD!

**"Fight or flight":** the reaction that occurs in a body when faced with a sudden threat; it prepares you automatically to either fight or escape

**Pride:** a group of lions

**Spoor:** another name for tracks and stool (poop)

Lions rest about 20 hours each day to save energy for hunting.

▼▲▼▲▼▲▼▲▼▲▼▲▼▲▼▲▼▲▼▲▼▲▼▲▼▲▼▲▼

The lions were charging in bursts, tails twitching each time they paused. You know how a cat's tail looks when it's angry? It's like it has a string attached and somebody's flicking it around. Finally one cat stayed behind. Then a second lion stopped and finally, the last. We kept running backwards until we were far away and eventually stopped under the shade of a tree. The cats were still watching us, crouched down in classic lion attack mode, with their tails flipping back and forth. We hoped we were safe.

That's when the male lion disappeared over the side of the ravine! Seconds later he was up and over onto our side. He looked like a spitball being shot out of a straw, straight at us, his mane

flat back against his head. Lions can cover incredible distances in short periods of time and this one was on a full-out attack.

Fortunately, I carry a bear banger, which up to that point I had forgotten about. When you fire a bear banger, it makes a sound like a shotgun and shoots a shell that explodes in a big burst of white smoke. So, I pulled it out of my pocket and let the firing pin fly. The lion was 20 meters (65 ft.) away and the sound made him hesitate, but he kept charging. Then the shell exploded about 2 meters (7 ft.) over his head in a big "kaboom," and the lion screeched to a stop. He ran back toward the females who perked up and fell in behind him.

Finally, we turned around and ran. Arms pumping, hearts pounding, and mud flying, we ran to the eye of the spring. We got to the other side and flopped down under the shade of a big

Cubs weigh from 1 to 2 kilograms (2 to 4 lb.) at birth and are helpless; they remain dependent for at least 16 months.

# Killing Perfection

▼▲▼▲▼▲▼▲▼▲▼▲▼▲▼▲▼▲▼▲▼▲▼▲▼▲▼▲▼▲▼

Lions are the end result of 30 million years of evolutionary killing perfection. They only know one thing—how to hunt—and they do so with absolute skill. This puts them at the top of the food chain. However, lions compete with hyenas for this top position. When a hyena clan threatens a lion pride at its kill, the male lion will kill the dominant female hyena with ease. Hyenas know this, so they don't often try to steal a pride's kill if there is a male lion around. Female lions, who do all of the hunting but only get to eat leftovers after the males have eaten, put up with males because of the "protection-from-hyenas factor." If there isn't a male around, there's a good chance that everything killed by the females would be taken by hyenas.

Back at Secret Springs, in the male lion's mind we were like hyenas, and he had to take us out because that is his job. And I don't doubt that he would have killed all three of us in seconds.

**A lion's colors provide the perfect camouflage for hiding in shrubs and grass, waiting to surprise their prey.**

tree. As we compared shaking hands, we giggled hysterically for about half an hour.

When I look back, I see that my premonition was right. We *had* made a mistake. You see, we assumed that the females Garth saw heading off in the other direction were this male lion's pride because the previous year there had only been one group of lions hunting at Secret Spring. But that year there were four groups. Our quick assumption that we were safe almost cost us our lives. It wasn't a mistake we'd make again.

## BRIAN'S NOTES

The Bushmen, a group of Aboriginal people from southern Africa, once used sheer bravado to go in and steal a lion's kill by yelling and screaming and hitting the ground with sticks.

Sometimes lions that live in captivity have manes that are matted like Rastafarian hairdos. In the wild, their hair is constantly combed by walking through the bush.

A lion's roar can be heard as far away as 13 kilometers (8 mi.).

# An OUTBACK WALKABOUT

I've been to Australia three times over the years, but the first time has a special place in my memory. We landed in Sydney and, on our first night, stayed in a bed and breakfast downtown. Early in the morning, just as the sun was coming up, we heard a kookaburra—right there in downtown Sydney! The kookaburra's song sounds like *kookookookookikikikikakakak-akakowkowkowkow*. It's the call I used to hear watching *Gilligan's Island* on TV when I was growing up. When I went to Australia, I found out that kookaburras don't really live on remote Pacific islands. Show producers just used their call because it sounded tropical, I guess.

You might think of Australia as being filled

A female kangaroo (called a doe or flyer) is nearly always pregnant and has three kids developing at one time—an embryo in the womb, a baby (or joey) in her pouch, and an older baby at her heels.

with huge deserts, but there are also rainforests, temperate forests, and many different coastal environments, including marsh flats. We spent our first weeks in Australia exploring the coast, canoeing and visiting islands, where we saw shearwaters and our first penguins, and then headed into the deserts of the interior.

Dee and I didn't have much money, so we bought a bus pass and headed toward Alice Springs in Central Australia. It was a 27-hour bus trip that was, in fact, very exciting. Every time I looked out the window there was something new to see. We passed through a town called Coober Pedy, where everybody lives underground because it's so hot. We saw lots of red sand, shrub land, and the occasional forest grove. I remember seeing huge buttes that had been eroded by wind, sand, and rain over thousands of years.

Every time we stopped for gas, we ran around looking for birds. I've

## BRIAN'S NOTES

A pair of kookaburras establishes a bond and strengthens it by singing. If one kookabura starts singing and its mate doesn't join in, then the bird slowly stops singing, sounding like a clock spring winding down.

When we climbed some of the peaks of the MacDonnell Ranges, we came across herds of camels and wild horses or "brumbies." The camels were brought over a century earlier. Now Australia exports camels to Arabia and other middle-eastern countries.

always said that if non-birdwatchers go to Australia, they'll become birdwatchers because the birds there are so colorful and abundant. We would make notes and then sit on the bus and page through our massive Australian bird book trying to identify what we'd seen—plumed pigeons, red-tailed and Major Mitchell cockatoos, Port Lincoln parrots, sacred kingfishers, crimson rosellas, and blue-faced honey-eaters, to name a few.

At Alice Springs we rented a car and headed out west to the MacDonnell Ranges in the Simpson Desert. We set up camp beside Ellery Gorge and then camped and hiked all over the

One of the most common parrots in eastern Australia, the crimson rosella, is also one of the most beautiful. Young birds are born almost completely green with a red cap, and gradually replace their green feathers with the crimson and blue ones of the adult.

region. Australia was where we learned how to hike in the heat. We brought big blocks of ice that we kept in Styrofoam coolers. We used the melting water to drink and to wet down our hats and shirts. With a wet shirt and hat, we could do anything in the heat, so we were able to hike incredible distances and experience some of the best of what the Simpson Desert has to offer.

Hiking in Australia's desert is like hiking through thousands of long-spined sea urchins thanks to spinifex grass, which is common in the outback and has thorns about as long as your index finger. It's tricky. You have to watch where you step, but you also want to watch what's around you so you don't miss anything.

Shaped by one of the oldest rivers in the world, Ellery Gorge offers visitors spectacular scenery and the occasional, cool, deep water hole or billabong as it's called in Australia.

# Shearwater Crash Site

▽▲▽▲▽▲▽▲▽▲▽▲▽▲▽▲▽▲▽▲▽▲▽▲▽▲▽▲▽

One afternoon on Phillip Island, just off the south coast of Australia, we visited a short-tailed shearwater nesting ground. Shearwaters are long-winged seabirds related to petrels that often skim close to the water surface. We walked carefully across the ground, which was covered with the holes these birds drill to build their nests underground. Sitting in the empty colony with our binoculars, we waited for sunset. Shearwaters always fly in after dark to avoid aerial predators, such as falcons.

Long past dark, we finally saw them—the water below us was thick with birds. In wave after wave, the shearwaters flew up toward us. Excellent flyers and gliders, they are not well adapted to life on land and they crashed, hitting the ground around us like snowballs. We were blown away by these avian rockets as we watched them disappear, scampering like rats going down a hole.

We got up early each morning and hiked until about eleven o'clock. Then we took a break from eleven until about four, while the heat was most intense. We'd spend our siesta beside the lagoon. It was beautiful—gorgeous blue water with blue skies above and red rock canyons on either side. We saw flocks of parrots and zebra finches as they visited the water for a drink. And because we were there during a near full moon, we could swim in the middle of the night. It was a strange experience to be treading water and to hear the sound of crickets and other desert night noises. It's some of the best camping we've ever done.

We met up with some friends at a place by the Murray River and they took us camping in a eucalyptus forest. Australia has hundreds of species of eucalyptus—all with that distinctive smell. The leaves contain oil that prevents other plants from growing nearby. This reduces competition for moisture, so the eucalyptus is able to survive quite nicely in the desert.

If there's one animal that says "Australia" to most of the world, it's the kangaroo. It seems like a storybook animal to us, but in Australia, kangaroos are common. We loved watching kangaroos and catching sight of joeys peeking out of pouches. I was in the tent early one morning when I heard a *doonk doonk doonk doonk*. There was a pause and then I heard the *doonk doonk doonk doonk* again. It was a kangaroo, right in our campsite. As I unzipped the tent to take a look, I heard *doonkdoonk-doonkdoonk* once more and saw the kangaroo disappear into the bush.

Despite the heat and the deserts, Australia's landscape is a friendly one that offers experiences you won't have anywhere else in the world. We were continually fascinated and thrilled with this environment of extremes, where everything has to work so hard to survive in such a flamboyant way!

**SAY THE WORD!**

**Aerial:** happening in the air

**Avian:** relating to birds

**Butte:** a high, steep-sided, flat-topped hill that rises suddenly from the surrounding area

# PETREL PUKE and HEADLESS KITTIWAKES

D ee and I love to travel in wilderness areas. This means we haven't spent much time in Europe, which has few remote wilderness areas left. But Dee's roots lie in Norway, so a recent family reunion gave us the chance to explore some of Norway's natural areas. We first spent a few weeks hiking Norway's beautiful Jotenheim National Park. The weather was typical for Europe's northern coast—cool temperatures, rain, mist, and fog.

We even woke up one morning to find wet snow blanketing our tent. Our views of the scenery were limited because of the fog, but we climbed two of Norway's highest peaks anyway.

Then by chance we came across a postcard of the Lofoten Islands. These jagged mountains sticking out of the ocean look like teeth in a dog's mouth. We had never heard of them before, but the islands looked so unusual that we were intrigued. So we rented a car, drove north, and took a ferry out to the islands, which were hidden by rain and mist. We climbed a peak in the fog and on the summit we could

**The Lofoten Islands, home to about 24,500 people, consist of some of the oldest rocks on earth. They provide for fantastic scenery and hiking.**

Banding birds, such as this small petrel, helps scientists collect information about their migration patterns, behavior, life-span, and survival rate.

barely see the ground below our feet. We were beginning to think that all the good views in Norway could only be found on postcards! And then the clouds started to lift, the weather cleared, and for the rest of our trip we experienced a cobalt blue sky.

One night we ate dinner at a restaurant that had window ledges wide enough to hold kittiwake nests. This was our first close encounter with kittiwakes, which are a delicate-looking gull. As we discovered once we reached Lofoten, the islands are famous for their nesting birds. For birdwatchers like Dee and me, this was great news. We made arrangements to be dropped off on an island with a huge kittiwake colony. Luckily, the sensitive time in the kittiwake nesting season had just ended, so it was legal to visit the island.

A boat delivered us and our camping gear to the base of an incredible cliff that was a 100 meters (330 ft.) tall. We were awestruck by the sights and sounds around us. Kittiwakes

## BRIAN'S NOTES

Puffins can carry several fish back to their nest at a time. The average catch is around 10 fish per trip, but the record is an amazing 62 fish at once! The puffin's beak is specialized to hold all these fish.

Petrel puke is actually called stomach oil and is a higly refined food for their young.

Seabirds often nest on islands and cliffs inaccessible to predators.

This young kittiwake had flown into a cave and become disoriented. When I discovered it, I carried it to the cave entrance where, after a few minutes, it was ready to spread its wings and fly.

were everywhere. They have a beautiful piercing call that we heard day and night during our stay. The sound will be forever embedded in my brain.

We explored the island, which was inhabited only by the birds, a few sheep, and us. We found a huge cave with a mouth that was about 50 meters (165 ft.) high. I walked into the darkness at the back and found a young kittiwake there that seemed disoriented.

It had likely flown in by accident. I carefully picked him up and walked to the cave opening. He was calm as a pet pigeon and just looked at me looking at him. Then he stood up, turned around, and looked outside the cave to get his bearings. Eventually he spread his wings and flew away.

In nature, where there is this much life there is also death. At one point a sea eagle flew in on the winds off the top of the cliff. We watched it float down like a kite, maybe a meter (3 ft.) away from the rock, freaking out the kittiwakes. As we watched, it reached out and plucked a youngster off the nest, as if it was pulling a grape off a vine. In a split second the eagle had snapped off the kittiwake's head. The eagle ate it on the wing and dropped the remains.

We also found intriguing bundles that looked like leather socks at the high-tide line. When we turned one of these "socks" inside out, we found the beak of a puffin. We realized with amazement that some predator was turning these birds inside out so that it

## SAY THE WORD!

**Fjord:** a long, narrow inlet of the sea between high cliffs

**Predator:** an animal that naturally eats other animals

**Zooplankton:** microscopic organisms that drift or float in the sea or fresh water

was easier to strip the body clean of meat.

Two biologists landed on our beach one day. They invited us to stay with them for a couple of nights on a nearby island where they were studying petrels—tiny black-and-white seabirds with webbed feet and a tubular bill. Petrels live on the open ocean and are probably the most abundant bird in the world. They eat by puddling their feet in the water to bring zooplankton to the surface.

I'll never forget holding these fragile little

birds with legs as thin as pencil leads. Their natural habitat—the open ocean—is a place you and I would consider violent, but the 10-meter (33-ft.) seas are a friendly place to petrels. They only come ashore for a couple of months a year to nest and then they're back out gliding over the open ocean.

We learned a lot about petrels during our stay with the biologists, including their

memorable defense mechanism—projectile vomiting. When you pick up a petrel, it spews whatever it's got in its gut. This lightens its weight so it can fly away more easily if it gets the chance to escape. We were quite surprised when we picked up a little bird and it opened its beak, squirting a foul-smelling fluid all over us. We call it petrel puke. It smells like something old, dead, and rotten—the worst-smelling substance you can imagine. Everywhere we went for the next few weeks, we could smell petrel puke on our clothes, even after washing them many times.

The common puffin, also known as the "sea parrot," has a distinctive bill which is red, blue-gray, and ivory during nesting season. The colors disappear when the nesting season ends.

I loved my visit to the Lofoten Islands, where I expected to see to see James Bond walk into my life at any moment! The incredible dog-toothed landscape and dramatic cliffs that were formed by the sea and the ice ages created a sense of adventure and mystery for me, which I still feel to the present day.

Among the smallest members of the gull family, kittiwakes are also the most oceanic. Unlike most gulls, they spend their lives at sea, except in the summer months, when they come ashore to nest.

# THINGS THAT FLY BY *in the* NIGHT

Giant river otters are four times the size of North American otters. They are found only in South America's most remote areas.

G uyana, which means "land of many waters," is one of the world's rare tropical countries that still has about 80 per cent of its rainforest intact. When you look at a map, you can see that the country is laced with wetlands, so building a road is tough stuff. The only road that goes into the Guyana interior can take 2 days to drive in good weather, or it can take 2 weeks in the rainy season, driving through puddles as deep as your vehicle. As a result, not many people live inland. Of the country's 700,000 inhabitants, only 5,000 live in the interior; everyone else lives on the coast.

Almost a third of all bat species have some form of a nose-leaf, the fleshy flap of skin above its nostrils that is believed to help with echolocation.

The highlight of our first trip to Guyana was a visit to Iwokrama, a wilderness reserve set aside in 1992 as Guyana's gift to the world's science community. Scientists from dozens of countries visit the research camp at Iwokrama to study rainforest environments. The camp is situated beside a large river that flows through the middle of 3,700 square kilometers (2,300 sq. mi.) of pristine rainforest. That river was our highway into the rainforest.

It isn't easy, hiking and birdwatching in the tropical forest. When you're on the forest floor, it's a bit like being in my basement—it's dark, damp, and dingy and there don't seem to be many interesting things to look at. If you go into the rainforest with an untrained eye or without a guide, you might wonder what all the fuss is about. However, if you're a biologist and know how to look for neat things, then there are amazing sights to be seen, especially 30 meters (100 ft.) above you in the forest canopy, where most of the action is happening.

The rainforest canopy is like the upstairs of

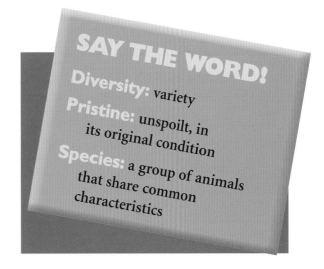

**SAY THE WORD!**

**Diversity:** variety

**Pristine:** unspoilt, in its original condition

**Species:** a group of animals that share common characteristics

my house, where you find colorful paintings, chandeliers, nice glassware, and more. Similarly, the forest canopy is where you find flocks of parrots, toucans, interesting monkeys, dainty hummingbirds, and beautiful orchids in bloom.

To really appreciate the rainforest, you need to get to the "upstairs" part of the "house." In rainforest regions around the world, local tourist industries have built canopy platforms and walkways for easy access. But if you don't have a platform or walkway nearby, then the best way to see a rainforest is from a river.

We returned to Guyana 2 years after our first visit, guiding a group of tourists. We traveled with them down the Burro Burro River as part of a tourism project that benefits the locals.

Of the eight hundred bats, or some fifty species, that the researchers had caught at Iwokrama, only one was a vampire bat. A balanced natural ecosystem has very few vampire bats; more can be found wherever people and farm animals live.

The Iwokrama Forest animal population consists of at least 200 species of mammals, 500 birds, 420 fish, and 150 reptiles and amphibians. More than 30 per cent of the mammals living in the Iwokrama Forest are listed as endangered.

Mist nets are very fine nets that look like spider webs. They are draped loosely in the forest and birds or bats fly into them, becoming harmlessly entangled. Scientists check the nets regularly—about every half hour—and carefully remove the trapped creatures. After making notes about the species that they find, they release the animals.

One night during our visit, researchers had set up nets at different elevations in the forest. Some nets were raised on pulley systems, 30 meters (100 ft.) up in the forest canopy, because certain species of bats fly only at

Researcher Burton Lim focuses on searching out rare mammals in Guyana, especially bats. On one expedition he saw twenty-six different species of bats, including fruit-eaters, nectar-feeders, insect-eaters, frog-eaters, and vampires.

that elevation. Other bat species only fly near the forest floor, so nets were located down low, too. We stopped off at the researchers' camp, put on headlamps, and walked along a trail with the scientists to the net locations. Every time we took down a net, we didn't know what we were going to find—it was as exciting as opening a pile of presents!

Plants that usually grow at the canopy top often grow downward to use the available light at the edge of the river. The result? Canopy species right at eye level! It is a great pleasure to get into a boat and paddle or float along silently and watch for wildlife, especially at sunrise or sunset, when the rainforest comes alive.

The best part of being in Iwokrama was working with a group of scientists who were setting up mist nets to help identify and catalogue species flying in the black of night.

Worldwide there are about a thousand bat species. In Canada there are only about eighteen species, because we live on the northern edge of

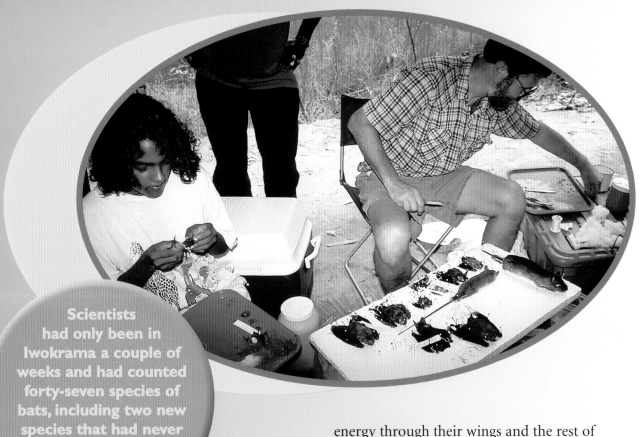

Scientists had only been in Iwokrama a couple of weeks and had counted forty-seven species of bats, including two new species that had never been recorded in Guyana before.

where bats can survive. Most bats fly here to take advantage of our good insects in the summer and then migrate to warmer regions in the winter.

In the tropics, where bats have evolved in a stable, warm environment, their numbers have exploded. Iwokrama's bats were amazing. One of the bats we caught that night had a big, chunky body—imagine a fat hamster with wings. Its wingspan was almost half a meter (1.6 ft.) long.

Big bats can survive in tropical areas because their big wings act like radiators giving off heat. This helps them stay relatively cool in hot, humid environments. This is also why bats get smaller and smaller as you go farther north—because of the colder climate, northern bats can't afford to lose too much of their heat energy through their wings and the rest of their body.

Iwokrama is an environmental hot spot—a place on the planet where there is a high diversity of species. These hot spots are places that the world conservation community targets for preservation. Guyana, because of its inaccessibility to people, has an opportunity to preserve large tracts of its forest. An important part of the Iwokrama philosophy is also figuring out a way for locals to make a living without damaging this rare environment.

Our experiences with the people and bats of Iwokrama were incredible. The remoteness of the rainforests of Guyana also made a very big impression on us. Not long after arriving in Guyana, we flew over the rainforest in a small plane for about an hour and a half and saw no signs of people below us. We could hardly believe our eyes, but we could still imagine the jaguars, tapirs, river otters, toucans, parrots, and all of the other amazing animals that exist in this place, undisturbed by humans!

# A TON *of* WRINKLES

Ellesmere Island is Canada's northern-most island. When I was 21 years old, I worked at the Eureka weather station on Ellesmere for 4 months. The other people at the station joked that my job was the "lowest in the Arctic." I did the things nobody else wanted to do—washed the dishes and floors, cleaned the urinals, and did odd repairs.

But I secretly knew I really had the best job in the Arctic. I had the most freedom of anyone at the station. I could work ahead sometimes and take off for 2 or 3 days to explore the island. In total, I probably hiked around 800 kilometers (500 mi.) that summer.

Eureka is located about 1,000 kilometers (620 mi.) south of the North Pole and about 2,000 kilometers (1,240 mi.) north of the nearest tree. The wide-open space of the arctic tundra surrounded me, which was pretty impressive for a kid used to the city. And interesting things happened. For example, once I was out by myself at two in the morning when a group of three wolves came over the ridge. I sat and watched them for a while and then I don't know what overcame me, but I howled—right at them. And you know what? One wolf sat down, pointed his muzzle at the sky, and answered me with a howl of his own. This was

A walrus's eyes become more bloodshot the longer it sits out on the ice. The veins in its eyes help get rid of excess heat.

I only slept in my tent once because I didn't want to waste an arctic night. If the huff of a walrus woke me, I could see it right away from where I slept outdoors without having to unzip the tent.

This musk ox skull was an exciting find. It allowed me to examine its trademark thick, curved horns. In a male, the horns meet at the top of its head, in what is called a "boss." Females have smaller horns, without a boss.

an exceptionally powerful moment for me! It was that summer on Ellesmere that planted a deep seed for my desire to explore wilderness areas.

About 5 years ago I joined a 2-week kayaking trip on the east side of Ellesmere. One day we kayaked up a fjord that is normally full of ice and discovered evidence of Inuit camps from about 500 years ago. We found piles of flint chips and could picture the Inuit, chipping away with their primitive stone tools. We also found abandoned fox traps, bits of arrowheads, and other stone tools. Every time we landed our kayaks, there were signs that the Inuit had landed there in the distant past. In a few places we could put our kayaks up on rock structures that were built 1,000 years ago to keep skin kayaks away from dogs' teeth. The area was truly rich with cultural history.

Hares go through a "boom and bust" cycle. The year I was on Ellesmere, when I was twenty-one, I could crawl into groups of three hundred hares. The next year there were hardly any to be found on the island.

And in many of the places we visited, there were green areas—places where perhaps 2,000 years' worth of seals had been skinned. Their blood had soaked into the soil and left nutrients that helped plants survive and thrive. And where there were plants, there were arctic hares, musk ox, and ptarmigan.

This wealth of cultural history and wildlife in the area is due to the presence of a polynya— a place of plenty. There are only about a half dozen polynyas in the Canadian Arctic. They are located where warm-water upwellings keep areas of the ocean free from ice and snow, and also supply nutrients that feed tiny organisms, which in turn feed fish. Fish then attract animals such as seals, sea ducks, and whales. And these animals are what brought the original Inuit to the region.

Walruses are creatures I find especially fascinating and bizarre—buck-toothed animals the size of grand pianos, wrapped in wrinkled burlap. They have long whiskers, which they use to find food. Imagine this huge creature diving deep in the cold, pitch-black arctic water and then mucking around on the ocean floor for molluscs the size of softballs. The whiskers are attached to nerve endings that are as sensitive as your lips. And their broad muzzles hide a mouth shaped like a half moon.

## BRIAN'S NOTES

When threatened, Arctic hares stand up on their hind legs and hop away like a kangaroo, reaching speeds up to 50 kilometers (31 mi.) per hour. They move so quickly that their enemies, wolves and foxes, have a hard time keeping up with them.

Musk oxen have been around since the last ice age when mastodons and mammoths still roamed the earth. Their underwool, called qiviut, is believed to be the world's warmest natural fiber and is as soft as cashmere.

Once the whiskers locate a mollusc, this "moon" sucks it in, removes the guts, and then spits out the shell. A walrus eats about 20 kilograms (44 lb.) of mollusc guts a day.

We saw walrus almost every day on our trip. Our goal was to kayak in close, spend some quiet time with the walrus, and then paddle away without scaring the animals into the water. So, whenever we approached a group of walrus on an ice floe, we would always make sure they saw us first, from a distance. We would just sit there, kayaks pulled together, making sure none of us had cameras with film that was about to run out. The whirring sound of an automatic camera rewinding would likely scare the walrus into the water.

Once we were sure that the walrus had seen us, we stuck together and kayaked toward them very slowly. Nobody spoke. Sometimes we got as close as 10 meters (33 ft.) and would watch them watch us. They looked at us with tired eyes like they didn't have a care in the world. We were probably some of the first people they'd ever seen—maybe even the first—so they didn't fear us. In areas where walrus are hunted, they are sometimes aggressive toward people.

Once we watched a walrus scratching an itch so vigorously that he started rocking the ice he was on and finally tipped another walrus into the water! Walrus seem to want to touch each other and are often found in a big huddle. One of the Inuit words for a group of walrus means "an ugly." And walrus are truly so ugly, they are appealing.

I have returned to the high Arctic several times since that first magical summer so many years ago and I never get tired of visiting and exploring the vast open spaces in the land of the midnight sun. Because the Arctic is an important and unique part of our country, I wish all Canadians could travel north once in a lifetime, to experience the amazing landscape and the creatures that make it home.

Although many wolf populations are threatened in the wild, the white-coated Arctic wolf is not; it lives farther north than most people do, so it is relatively safe from hunting and habitat destruction.

# *The* PENGUIN SUPERHIGHWAY

Most people love penguins because they're so incredibly cute. And each penguin species has its own fascinating behavior that adds to its charm.

One penguin activity I love to watch is pebble stealing, which occurs constantly in colonies of chinstrap penguins. Chinstraps build their nests out of pebbles. You'll often see them approaching each other's nests to nab a pebble or two. If the nest-owner notices that one of its pebbles is about to be stolen, it will protest loudly until the would-be thief leaves to find a less watchful penguin.

Penguins steal pebbles so they can make their own nests a little better. The higher they can get their nests off the ground, the less chance there is for their eggs to be frozen or waterlogged in a quick melt in the summer. Researchers have put a pile of colored pebbles in a penguin colony and then kept track of where the pebbles go. They've found that the stones migrate all over the colony as they are stolen and re-stolen from nest to nest.

Penguins are oceanic birds. They only come ashore a few months out of

**Icebergs in the Antarctic assume many fantastic shapes as the result of erosion, thawing, melting, and bumping into each other.**

26

Penguins evolved around 100 million years ago when their ancestors gave up flying in favor of swimming in the sea, with its rich food sources.

the year to nest. The rest of the time they're out in the open ocean—traveling far and wide. Some penguins live in tropical areas that have cold oceanic currents. You can find them right on the Equator! I've been snorkeling in the waters off the Galapagos Islands, bobbing along like a cork, and had a little bullet zip by me in pursuit of fish, leaving only a trail of air bubbles. A penguin's wings, useless above ground, are the perfect propulsion tools underwater, where penguins "fly."

But the penguin story I want to tell you happened on the last day of a trip I took into the Antarctic in 2002. We had already visited several penguin populations, but I had never dreamed of a colony of the size that we were about to see.

We were at a place called Deception Island, and the seas were calm. We got into our small boats, called Zodiacs, and went ashore. As we approached the black lava beach, we noticed there was nothing but penguins as far as we could see. Every wave that rolled in brought penguins with it. And every wave that went out took penguins away.

As we bailed out of the boats and made our way to higher ground, I saw an endless parade of chinstrap penguins waddling to the sea and another waddling back from the ocean to their nests. The penguins heading to the ocean were

## SAY THE WORD!

**Crest:** to reach the top or crest of a hill

**Krill:** tiny shelled animals found in seas around the Antarctic, a nutritious food source for a variety of Antarctic creatures

**Regurgitate:** to bring swallowed, partly digested food back up into the mouth; birds often regurgitate food to feed their young

**Our guide estimated that there were about 200,000 king penguins in this colony on the ice-free slopes of the rocky South Georgia Island coast.**

▼▲▼▲▼▲▼▲▼▲▼▲▼▲▼▲▼▲▼▲▼▲▼▲▼▲▼▲▼▲▼

often dirty because they had been sitting on their nests for a while. Now their stomachs were empty, and they were going to hunt for krill to feed to their youngsters. The penguins heading back from the water were returning with their tummies full to take a turn on the nest. I was reminded of the hustle and bustle of the city during rush hour, except this "city" was in one of the most remote places in the world. And we were the only ones not wearing a tuxedo.

We soon realized that the penguins were heading toward a narrow valley farther inland and decided to follow them. It was like a double-lane highway with half the penguins moving out of the colony and the other half moving in. We found ourselves walking in a river of penguins about thirty waddlers wide, taking tiny, penguin-sized steps. I had the feeling that I love when I get into natural settings I've never experienced before—a feeling of overwhelming excitement.

As we walked through the opening valley, we crested a hill and had a great view of the scene before us. And as far as we could see, all the way to the basin's ridge, more than a kilometer (0.6 mi.) away, there was nothing but penguins— probably 200,000 of them. Although it was snowing quite hard, I lay on my belly in the penguin poop and melting snow. Dee held an umbrella over me as I videotaped the penguins marching past. I could hear their toenails clicking on the hard, packed soil. It sounded like the pitter-patter of rain.

Occasionally one or two of the penguins would come over to me and look right into the lens. It was as if they were trying to see if my camera was a Sony or a Canon! And then they continued on past because, of course, they all had a mission.

All around us we could see penguin families reuniting, which is an impressive accomplishment when you think about it. Imagine finding your parents in a crowd of thousands of people who look exactly the same as they do. This is how the penguins do it. Adults go to the approximate area where they last saw their youngster and start to call. A youngster recognizes its parent's voice and calls back. Parents and youngsters continue calling until they find each other. Then the adult regurgitates some krill into the mouth of its child.

We could also see adult pairs reuniting with an ecstasy call. Whenever a chinstrap mate returns to the nest, both penguins point their little beaks to the sky, stick their wings out, and flap them back and forth with a little cry. So at any given time when you're watching a chinstrap colony, you can see ecstasy calls happening all around you. Chinstrap penguin couples help maintain their lifelong bond with this lovely call.

It was with great reluctance that we finally admitted to ourselves that it was time to leave. Just being on land away from our boat was a very risky deal because the wind could change suddenly and bring a storm that could prevent us from leaving shore. So eventually, back we went to our Zodiacs, walking ever so slowly and keeping company with the penguins who were streaming back down to the ocean for a bite to eat.

The best way to view penguins, such as these magnificent king penguins, is to quietly slip into their colonies and get right down at eye level.

Gentoo penguins, with their tell-tale orange beaks, often argue with their neighbors, especially at nest-building time when they are competing for nesting materials.

Although known as Wallace's flying frog, this species actually glides between trees or from the tree canopy down to the ground using the webbing between its toes as miniature parachutes.

# The LAND of LIGHT BULB NOSES

D ee and I are fascinated by the great apes because they are a mirror reflection of who people are. We had been to see mountain gorillas on several occasions and had traveled to Tanzania to see chimpanzees with Jane Goodall. Next, we wanted to see orangutans. So we went to Borneo, one of the only places in the world you can observe them in the wild. Orangutans are often difficult to find. You have to watch and listen carefully because orangutans will watch you walk by and won't make a sound.

While we were in Borneo, it was another

Proboscis monkeys have a beautiful coat of beige, reddish brown, and white. They look like they are dressed in three-piece pajamas.

primate that caught my attention —the proboscis monkey, found only in Borneo.

Male proboscis monkeys are amazing-looking creatures. They have a nose like a light bulb, hanging between their eyes. And the older they get, the bigger their nose gets. Some older males actually have to hold their noses up to push food into their mouths. An elderly male's nose can reach 17.5 centimeters (9 in.) in length, which is about a quarter of his body length. People have asked, what is that nose for? Attracting females! A big nose tells a female proboscis that the male is old, experienced, and a survivor. This makes him a good monkey to team up with.

Proboscis monkeys have huge potbellies with a stomach like a cow's. This stomach is specially adapted to digest tough plants, such as the leaves proboscis monkeys thrive on. Because they can eat leaves, the most abundant food source on the planet, proboscis monkeys survive in places where other monkeys cannot.

Mangrove leaves are a very important part of the proboscis monkey's diet. They are found on trees that live in coastal areas, where fresh water streams into the ocean.

Because their main food grows in water, the proboscis is one of the few primates that can swim. Its toes are even somewhat webbed. The proboscis monkey is also an excellent leaper and will try to jump from tree to tree, but occasionally it makes a mistake or a branch breaks, and then it falls into the water. If this happens, it can easily swim to shore, but it had better watch out for crocodiles!

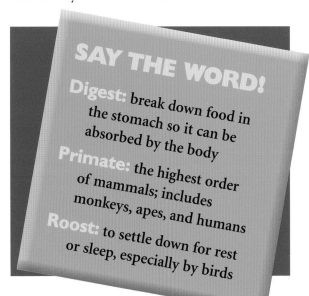

Walking along the suspension bridge that formed part of an exciting "canopy walk" gave us a bird's-eye view of the amazing Borneo jungle. It was an unforgettable experience.

Dee and I went to Bako National Park and hiked into the forest in search of proboscis monkeys. We saw our first ones fairly quickly, but they were very shy. Whenever I caught a glimpse of one, it was always already looking at me and a second later it would be gone. We spent 3 days hiking in incredible heat and humidity searching for proboscis monkeys, and hardly saw them at all.

## SAY THE WORD!

**Digest:** break down food in the stomach so it can be absorbed by the body

**Primate:** the highest order of mammals; includes monkeys, apes, and humans

**Roost:** to settle down for rest or sleep, especially by birds

Borneo's populations of proboscis monkeys are separated by great distances. In some places, there are only about 150 monkeys in a single area.

helping the proboscis monkeys to survive.

To our surprise, we came across a troop of proboscis monkeys right at the end of the day. They were moving across a channel of water, probably going to their favorite tree to roost for the night. We watched them climb onto a branch and use their body weight to bounce back and forth to get some momentum. Then suddenly they would release and catapult off the branch with arms and legs flailing. And bang! They would be onto another branch, which would sag under their weight. The proboscis are chunky monkeys—males can

We then headed to the province of Sabah on Borneo's southeast coast to look for a special group of elephants. They are small—males are just 2.6 meters (8.5 ft.) tall and females, only 2 meters (6.6 ft.). Locals call them "Disney elephants" because they look like toy animals. We found a group of elephants eating the rich grasses in a clearing along the river's edge. They looked like they were standing in a salad bowl.

We climbed out of our boat and moved through mud up to our knees to reach higher ground so we could watch them up close. We were amazed at how often the elephants trumpeted to keep in touch with each other. They sounded like upset African elephants, but we learned that these elephants make loud sounds so they can be heard through the thick rainforest vegetation of their habitat. There are only about 2,000 of these elephants left on the island. The government is trying to protect them with parks, which is also

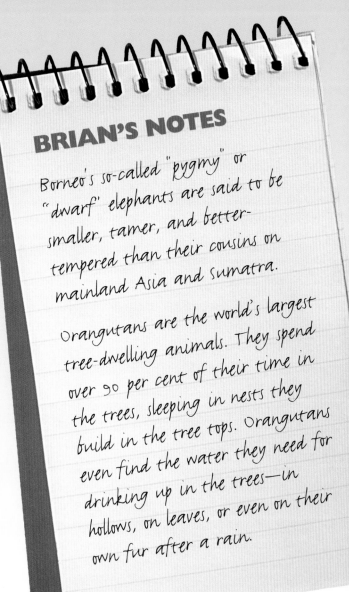

**BRIAN'S NOTES**

Borneo's so-called "pygmy" or "dwarf" elephants are said to be smaller, tamer, and better-tempered than their cousins on mainland Asia and Sumatra.

Orangutans are the world's largest tree-dwelling animals. They spend over 90 per cent of their time in the trees, sleeping in nests they build in the tree tops. Orangutans even find the water they need for drinking up in the trees—in hollows, on leaves, or even on their own fur after a rain.

# Mangroves and the Ocean Fishery

Mangrove trees are found in tropical areas around the world and are important to coastal regions. The trees hold soil and beach together, and prevent erosion of the land. But we've only recently discovered how important mangroves are to the world's ocean fishery. Mangroves provide a place for oceanic fish to lay their eggs. Without mangroves, there wouldn't be an ocean fishery. But mangroves are disappearing all over the world because of the world's appetite for inexpensive prawns. Prawns thrive in dyked-in areas around mangroves. Thus, the prawn industry is destroying many mangrove forests.

Although Borneo faces some of these threats, the government knows that proboscis monkeys attract tourists, so they've recently protected many of their mangrove forests by creating nature reserves.

be 21 kilograms (46 lb.) and the females, 10 kilograms (22 lb.).

As we watched, the male was first to cross. He then sat on a half-submerged log and encouraged his troop to follow by moving his head back and forth quickly, barking, and honking loudly. Apparently female proboscis monkeys find this noise soothing. As the females jumped and flew through the air, we would sometimes see little babies clinging to their mother's body. It looked like they were stuck on with Velcro.

All that work in Bako, searching for days for proboscis monkeys, and here they were in Sabah, putting on a dramatic show when we least expected it! It was a highlight of our trip and reminded us once again that nature works in mysterious but wonderful ways, surprising and delighting us wherever we go!

This beautiful, large pitcher plant is carnivorous which means it attracts, captures, and digests insects and other small creatures!

# LOOKING INTO *the* EYES *of* GODZILLA

The Galapagos Islands should be deserted. They are 1,000 kilometers (620 mi.) off the coast of Ecuador, which is much too far for mainland animals to easily reach by swimming. However, every now and then, a few creatures and plants somehow ended up on their shores. In relative isolation, these creatures evolved fascinating behaviors, shapes, and sizes. So, far from being deserted, the Galapagos Islands are home to hundreds of unusual plants and animals.

The most famous of the Galapagos's creatures is the giant tortoise. In the nineteenth century, the islands hosted about a quarter of a million tortoises. Unfortunately for the tortoises, they were a cheap, easy source of food for whalers. Tortoise meat would last a long time without freezing or drying because whalers kept tortoises alive in the bottom of their ships until they were ready to eat them. Up to 250 giant tortoises disappeared every time a whaling boat visited

Sometimes there are so many iguanas on the beach, warming their cold little bodies after a dive, that they climb on top of one another to get the best sun.

The giant tortoise, which can weigh up to 200 kilograms (440 lb.) and live from 100 to 150 years, gave its name to the Galapagos Islands—"galapago" means tortoise in Spanish.

the islands. By the mid twentieth century, they were almost extinct.

Fortunately, the Charles Darwin Research Station has a successful captive breeding program for giant tortoises. There are now about fifteen thousand giant tortoises on the islands.

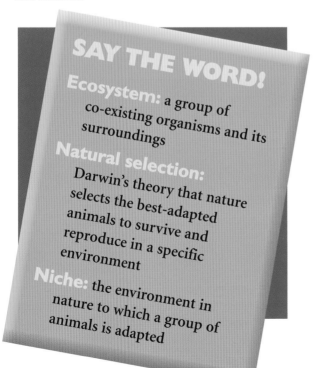

SAY THE WORD!

Ecosystem: a group of co-existing organisms and its surroundings

Natural selection: Darwin's theory that nature selects the best-adapted animals to survive and reproduce in a specific environment

Niche: the environment in nature to which a group of animals is adapted

The Galapagos creature I find the most fascinating is the iguana. The Galapagos is the place to enjoy iguanas. There are about seventy species worldwide, only one of which swims in the ocean and feeds on seaweed—the Galapagos marine iguana. Somehow this lizard has figured out a way to make a living on seaweed. And it swims in the ocean, which is even more remarkable for a cold-blooded animal. Remember that cold-blooded animals need to keep their bodies warm for blood circulation.

Every day when the high tide went out, we would see a mass of iguanas crawling toward the water. Some kind of mechanism kicks into place when the tide changes that makes them all head for the water at once.

Marine iguanas really look like prehistoric monsters. They can be a meter long (3 ft.) or more, but most are half that length. Once they've swum out to a seaweed bed, they dive. Hanging onto underwater lava rock with their razor-sharp claws, they feed quickly on the fast-growing seaweed. They come to within a hair's

The Galapagos land iguanas have a good thing going with Darwin's finches, which help them get rid of the ticks on their bodies by eating them.

Now and again when we were snorkeling, we were lucky enough to see an iguana swim by us. A friend of mine has a story about scuba diving and holding onto some underwater lava while taking pictures. When he looked down, he saw an iguana holding onto his arm as it chewed seaweed! It was a surprise, but not frightening. Marine iguanas are harmless.

Because iguanas eat seaweed, you can imagine how much salt they take into their bodies. All mammals have to figure out a way to get rid of excess salt, especially animals that live in ocean breadth of being too cold to survive and then they swim back to the beach.

Marine iguanas have black skin that helps them absorb heat and sunlight so they can warm up quickly. The black lava rock beaches of the Galapagos also absorb the sun's heat beautifully and get very hot. You know how, at the movie theatre, kids (never you) have squished bubble gum flat on the underside of a chair? That's what the iguanas look like on the beach. They spread their little arms out and squish their bellies, chins, and tails against the hot rock. You can almost hear them sighing in relief. Once their bodies are warm again, their stomach juices start to digest the seaweed.

Sometimes there are so many iguanas trying to warm themselves that they pile on top of each other. It's a strange sight—like someone took baskets full of laundry and dumped them on the beach.

## BRIAN'S NOTES

The classic term for a group of turtles (or tortoises) is a bale—a "bale of turtles."

Giant tortoises are the longest-lived of all vertebrates (animals with backbones). They can live for at least 100 years and they may live for up to 200 years. If that is true, then today's visitors to the islands may be seeing the very same tortoises that Darwin did when he visited in the early 1800s!

environments. For example, a gull has special glands in its face that extract salt from its blood. The salt concentrates in a drop on the end of its beak. Every now and then the gull shakes its face and the drop flies off.

Iguanas have to do the same thing. They have a specialized way to extract salt from their bodies and concentrate it in nose droplets. Sometimes when you're down on your belly looking out at a beach of iguanas, you'll see one move its head toward the sky and blow the salty white snot out its nose.

Everything about lizards fascinates me. When I look into the eyes of a lizard, I think of Godzilla, the monster lizard of movie fame.

But swimming with real lizards—the very

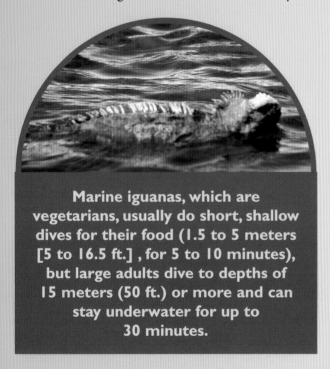

**Marine iguanas, which are vegetarians, usually do short, shallow dives for their food (1.5 to 5 meters [5 to 16.5 ft.] , for 5 to 10 minutes), but large adults dive to depths of 15 meters (50 ft.) or more and can stay underwater for up to 30 minutes.**

cool Galapagos marine iguanas—is a thousand times better than seeing Godzilla in a movie. There is no comparison. And I will never forget that lava rock beach in the Galapagos Islands that was paved with mini-Godzillas—a sea of tiny prehistoric monsters minding their own business, simply trying to warm up in the sun.

# The Famous Galapagos Finch

Charles Darwin, the naturalist on the HMS *Beagle*, was just 22 years old when he visited the Galapagos in the early 1800s. While visiting the Galapagos, he began to study the amazing finches on the islands. All finches are similar, he observed, but there were clearly different groupings, or species. Some finches live on the ground. Others live in trees. Some eat seeds. Others eat plants. One eats the prickly pear cactus. And another uses a twig or cactus spine to probe tree bark for insects. The most amazing one, I think, is the vampire finch. It nicks the skin of baby birds and drinks the resulting droplets of blood. It was through his study of Galapagos finches that Darwin concluded that all the finches had a common ancestor. From there he later developed his theory that species evolve (change) over time to fit specific environmental niches. Darwin's theories began a scientific revolution. His book, *The Origin of Species by Means of Natural Selection*, is still studied by biologists today.

# POGO STICK PUPS

The first time I saw a wild dog was on one of my first trips to Africa. We were walking through tall grass at the crack of dawn, looking for wildlife. Suddenly our guide called "Wild dog!" I whipped my binoculars up, looked across the grass, and there was a head. And then it was gone. And then the head was there again. The dog kept jumping up to get a look at us over the grass—it was as if he was on a pogo stick.

We call them wild dogs, but they're really the equivalent of African wolves—calico-colored wolves. Some people have started calling them African painted dogs to tell them apart from domestic dogs gone wild.

Wild dogs usually hunt in packs of ten, although packs can be larger or smaller. Their main prey is the impala, which is about the size of a small deer. Wild dogs feed cooperatively, with little or no growling. And they feed quickly. When a pack pulls down an impala, it eats the whole animal in about half an hour.

Wild dogs are thinly built, like greyhounds. They trot continuously and seem to walk on their tippy toes with a distinctive prance.

Wild dogs mainly hunt impala—maybe 80 to 90 per cent of their prey is impala. The impala is the same size as a small deer and weighs about 45 kilograms (100 lb.).

By the time we reached the spot where we'd seen the wild dog jumping up and down, there was just a skeleton left. The pack had finished its prey and moved on. I was intrigued. I wanted to see wild dogs again, but it was years before I would.

My best wild dog experience happened in Zimbabwe at the Save Nature Conservancy, Africa's wild dog sanctuary. One day we got up at about 4:30 in the morning, in the cold and dark, and drove to a small hill where the dogs had recently been seen. It was a dismal day.

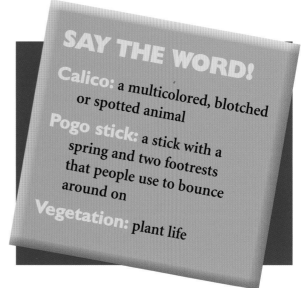

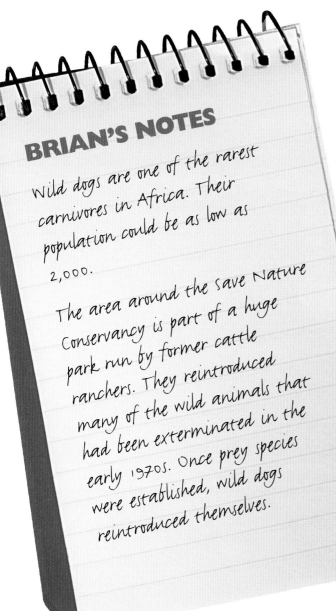

## BRIAN'S NOTES

Wild dogs are one of the rarest carnivores in Africa. Their population could be as low as 2,000.

The area around the Save Nature Conservancy is part of a huge park run by former cattle ranchers. They reintroduced many of the wild animals that had been exterminated in the early 1970s. Once prey species were established, wild dogs reintroduced themselves.

We waited, and waited, and waited in the cold, but nothing happened. Gradually, a few birds started singing and Africa woke up. Then we heard the yelp of a wild dog in the distance.

In wild dog society, adults leave the den about an hour or so before sunrise. Under the cover of darkness, they head out to hunt. The pack was now on its way back to the den, bellies full of food.

With my binoculars, I could see at least two dish-eared dogs looking our way. Although they were used to vehicles, they were still cautious as they approached. We started picking out more and more dogs, until we counted nine. One of them came right past us. It was the lead female. She trotted into some nearby vegetation and shortly we heard the barking, yelping, and squealing of puppies. A moment later, the female reappeared, followed by eight little puppies trotting in single file.

The pups started jumping up, licking the faces of the adults, trying to coax them to regurgitate some food. You know how your dog is always trying to lick your face? These aren't kisses as much as they are a request for a snack! Your dog is hoping you'll regurgitate some of your last meal to

A wild dog's ears are always on the move, listening for prey. Wild dogs kill from 80 to 85 per cent of what they chase. Lions kill only 20 per cent, if that!

share. Finally, one of the adults circled around, found a good spot, leaned over, and barfed up the morning's impala. The puppies pounced. They gathered around the puddle of food like the spokes of a wheel around a hub and ate with enthusiasm. In turn, adult after adult brought up a bit of food for the youngsters, until they'd all had their fill.

After the meal, the puppies grew curious about us. Our cameras were clicking as the little bright-eyed pack moved toward our vehicles. They got to within a few meters and then ran back to the adults.

We sat with the dogs for two days. As we got to know the pack members, we learned the story of Porridge, who was named by a park researcher. One of Porridge's back feet had been caught in a poacher's snare, and although she had broken free, her foot had been seriously damaged. She eventually chewed her

own foot off above the heel because it hurt so much. As a result, she walked with a limp and never hunted with the pack.

In hyena or lion society, Porridge would long since have died. But wild dogs tolerate their injured relatives. The dogs not only allowed her to stay with the pack, but also made her the official babysitter. One adult has to stay behind with the pups when the rest go to hunt. This became Porridge's full-time job. She ate by begging for food from the other adults. Porridge survived for 2 years doing this, but, sadly, was eventually killed by a car on a road.

Porridge's story is an example of the kind of tragedy humans can create in the animal world. In Africa, wild dog numbers have fallen drastically through hunting. Like wolves in other parts of the world, wild dogs have a bad name among ranchers as killers of livestock.

Wild dogs are very social. The den site is full of touching, licking, head butting, and play.

While it is true some wild dogs bring down livestock, not all do. Still, wild dogs have been persecuted and killed because of it. And hunting isn't the only threat for wild dogs. They are also dying from diseases passed on by domestic dogs that haven't been vaccinated against distemper and rabies.

But changes are happening. In general, the more people learn about wild animals, the less they feel threatened by them. Posters about wild dogs have been hung up in schools, post offices, and shopping areas, and biologists have gone into schools to talk about the animals. The effort seems to be working.

Wild dog populations in Zimbabwe and Botswana are now stable, and tragic stories like Porridge's will hopefully become a thing of the past.

Spotted hyenas, along with lions and leopards, sometimes hunt and kill wild dogs and their pups. The competition between these top predators can be fierce!

41

# SAVING GHANA'S HIPPOS

**A hippo's eyes, ears, and nose are all found on the top of its head so it can see, hear, and breathe while staying mostly underwater.**

In June 2001, Dee and I went to Ghana, a country on West Africa's coast, to visit the Wechiau Hippo Sanctuary, which is in a remote, northern part of the country. The Calgary Zoo Conservation Fund had been supporting the sanctuary for 5 years, and this was going to be our first time there.

The day after we arrived, the local chiefs invited us to a welcoming ceremony. It was an incredible experience—drumming, dancing, and all the bright African clothing you can imagine. As one of the chiefs gave his speech, he suddenly fell silent, then continued, "I just had a vision. I saw myself at the Calgary Zoo."

Honestly, I didn't think much about his comment at the time. But after our week at the sanctuary, I think it was Dee who said,

"Brian, you know, maybe the chief's vision was right. Maybe he should come to the Calgary Zoo." And of course, she was right because we were opening the biggest exhibit we'd ever opened—Destination Africa. The chiefs' presence at the opening would demonstrate the zoo's work in Ghana and its commitment to modern conservation methods.

In the water, hippo bulls will always defend their territory. Sometimes a younger bull will challenge the one in charge and a big battle takes place, leaving scars that last a lifetime.

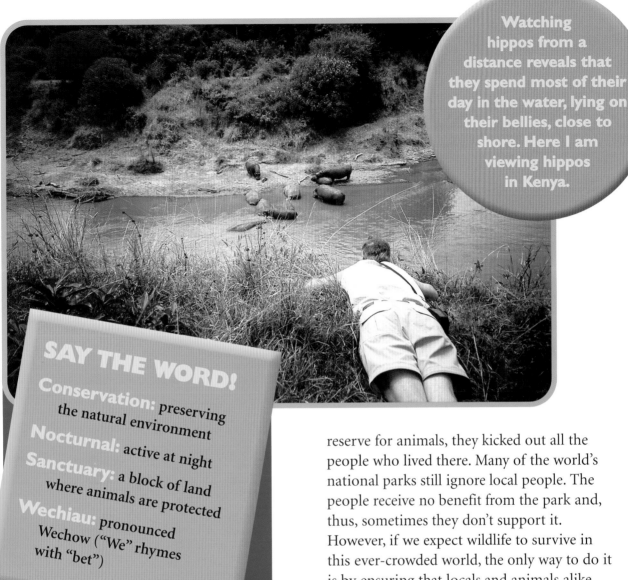

Watching hippos from a distance reveals that they spend most of their day in the water, lying on their bellies, close to shore. Here I am viewing hippos in Kenya.

**SAY THE WORD!**

**Conservation:** preserving the natural environment

**Nocturnal:** active at night

**Sanctuary:** a block of land where animals are protected

**Wechiau:** pronounced Wechow ("We" rhymes with "bet")

For thousands of years, zoos just took animals from the wild and put them in cages. We can't do that anymore because too many animals are close to extinction. Each animal removed from the wild could affect its species' survival. Hippos are almost extinct in West Africa. In Ghana there are only two populations. Luckily, one is protected by a national park and the other is protected by the Wechiau Hippo Sanctuary.

In the old days, when people made a park reserve for animals, they kicked out all the people who lived there. Many of the world's national parks still ignore local people. The people receive no benefit from the park and, thus, sometimes they don't support it. However, if we expect wildlife to survive in this ever-crowded world, the only way to do it is by ensuring that locals and animals alike prosper while living in or near a park.

The Wechiau Hippo Sanctuary is special because it's a Wechiau traditional area initiative, managed locally. And slowly the sanctuary is attracting tourists. Not very many—remember, it's in a very remote area of Ghana—but with each tourist comes much-needed money that benefits the village.

Three chiefs came to the Calgary Zoo in January 2003: Naa Imoru Nandom Gomah II, Naa Danyagiri Walaman-i Seubah II, and Naa Banda-naa Chielinah (Naa means "Your Highness" or "Chief"). One of the chiefs gave an absolutely riveting speech at the opening of the Destination Africa exhibit. He talked about how the sanctuary's hippo population was increasing in number and about why saving the hippos' habitat saves both hippos and many other animals.

When he finished his speech and turned away from the podium, the audience rose and applauded. The sound was so enthusiastic that it sent chills up my spine. And it just got better from there. We walked outside and one of the chiefs gave a blessing and cut the garland with a machete. It was the beginning of a new era in the relationship between the Calgary Zoo and the hippo sanctuary, but it was also a symbolic initiation into the conservation work zoos do today.

## BRIAN'S NOTES

A hippo's skin secretes a sticky pink fluid that protects the animal from dehydration, sunburn, and probably infection. This is likely the source of the myth that hippos sweat blood.

What looks like a yawn in hippos is actually a threat—a hippo's way of displaying its most fearsome weapons, its long, thick, sharp teeth.

Hippos are the third largest animal on land, after elephants and rhinos.

I enjoyed this "photo op" with the visiting chiefs from Ghana— (*left to right*) Naa Danyagiri Walaman-i Seubah II, Naa Banda-naa Chielinah, and Naa Imoru Nandom Gomah II. Naa means "Your Highness" or "Chief."

# A Night in the Hippo Sanctuary

Hippos are nocturnal. They spend their days in rivers and come out at night to feed on grasses. A farmer's field beside a river makes a tasty treat, but, for obvious reasons, farmers don't like that. To make the Wechiau Hippo Sanctuary successful, the local community decided to develop a "core" area for the hippos along the river's edge—a favorite hippo hangout—extending about 2 kilometers (1.2 mi.) inland. All farmers and fishing camps have moved outside the core, eliminating most of the region's conflicts between people and hippos.

The highlight of our visit to the sanctuary was spending the night on a platform in the rainforest's canopy. It was at the river's edge, about 10 meters (33 ft.) high, in a huge fig tree. We hauled mattresses onto the platform and put a mosquito net overtop. Then we crawled under the net and watched the sun set.

The tropical forest in Africa is a remarkable place. You can hear all kinds of weird noises: tree hyraxes screaming from distant areas, monkeys settling in to sleep for the night and, of course, fruit bats that visit the rainforest to eat. The moon was almost full, so we could watch the bats' silhouettes as they landed on the branches above us. Because the moon was so bright, birds sometimes broke into song in the middle of the night.

We also heard the slosh of hippos coming out of the river to eat. With their big, broad mouths, they just chomped, chomped, chomped all night long. Up in the canopy, we heard their lips crunching on the grass, pulling it into their mouths. They sounded like big, fat, wet conveyor belts.

Hippos eat a phenomenal amount of grass each night and are an important part of the food chain. For example, when you walk through the forest, you can see hippo poop 4 or 5 meters (13 or 16 ft.) up a tree. How can that be? You know hippos don't climb trees! However, when hippos poop, they shake their tail like a fan so it spreads the poop all over the place. It flies in every direction and sticks to all kinds of things. In the water, where hippos spend most of their time, their poop feeds small creatures that live there, which in turn feed the fish. Fishing in Africa is, therefore, at its best in ponds and rivers where hippos live.

# CONSERVATION—IT'S UP TO YOU!

If you'd like to learn more about or become involved in wildlife conservation, contact any or all of the following organizations.

**Calgary Zoo**
1300 Zoo Road, SE
Calgary, AB T2E 7V6
1-403-232-9333
www.calgaryzoo.ab.ca

**Canadian Parks and Wilderness Society**
National Office
880 Wellington Street, Suite 506
Ottawa, Ontario K1R 6K7
info@cpaws.org   1-800-333-WILD
www.cpaws.org

**Canadian Nature Federation**
1 Nicholas Street, Suite 606
Ottawa, Ontario K1N 7B7
cnf@cnf.ca        1-613-562-3447
www.cnf.ca

**Canadian Wildlife Federation**
350 Michael Cowpland Drive
Kanata, Ontario K2M 2W1
info@cwf-fcf.org  1-800-563-WILD
www.cwf-fcf.org

**Conservation of Arctic Flora and Fauna**
Hafnarstraeti 97
600 Akureyri, Iceland
caff@caff.is        www.caff.is

**David Suzuki Foundation**
2211 West 4th Avenue, Suite 219
Vancouver, BC V6K 4S2
solutions@davidsuzuki.org
1-800-453-1533
www.davidsuzuki.org

**Ducks Unlimited** (Wetland Conservation)
Box 1160
Oak Hammock Marsh, Manitoba R0C 2Z0
1-800-665-3835   www.ducks.ca

**Eastern Slopes Grizzly Bear Project**
Faculty of Environmental Design
University of Calgary
2500 University Dr. NW
Calgary, Alberta T2N 1N4
www.canadianrockies.net/grizzly

**The Jane Goodall Institute** (Canada)
Mr. Nicolas Billon, Executive Assistant
P.O. Box 477, Victoria Station
Westmount, Quebec  H3Z 2Y6
nicolas@janegoodall.ca     1- 514-369-3384 (fax)
www.janegoodall.ca

**Marmot Recovery Foundation**
Marmot
Box 2332, Station A
Nanaimo, BC V9R 6X9
1-877-4MARMOT   www.marmots.org

**Sable Island Green Horse Society**
c/o Zoe Lucas
P.O. Box 64, Halifax CRO
Halifax, Nova Scotia B3J 2L4
greenhorse@canada.com   www.greenhorsesociety.com

**World Wildlife Fund Canada**
245 Eglington Avenue E, Suite 410
Toronto, Ontario M4P 3J1
panda@wwfcanada.org   1-800-PANDA
www.wwfcanada.org

**Cool Sites on the Web:**
Species At Risk: **www.speciesatrisk.ca**
Space for Species: **www.spaceforspecies.ca**
Great Apes: **www.unep.org/grasp**
            **www.4apes.com**

# INDEX

We were lucky to see this orangutan mother and her baby when we were in Borneo. Young orangutans depend on their mothers longer than any other animal in the world. Male children stay until they are about 8 years old, but females stay into their teens so they can learn mothering skills.

Cover and interior design by John Luckhurst/GDL
All photos by Brian and Dee Keating, except p. 30
    (proboscis monkey) by Gayleen Jorgensen
Edited by Lauri Seidlitz
Proofread by Meaghan Craven
Scans by St. Solo Computer Graphics

The publisher gratefully acknowledges the support of The Canada Council for the Arts and the Department of Canadian Heritage.

THE CANADA COUNCIL | LE CONSEIL DES ARTS
FOR THE ARTS | DU CANADA
SINCE 1957 | DEPUIS 1957

We acknowledge the financial support of the Government of Canada through the Book Publishing Industry Development Program (BPIDP) for our publishing activities.

Printed in Hong Kong

05 06 07 08 / 5 4 3

First published in the United States in 2005 by Fitzhenry & Whiteside
121 Harvard Avenue, Suite 2
Allston, MA 02134

National Library of Canada Cataloguing in Publication

Keating, Brian, 1955–
    Going wild : amazing animal adventures around the world / Brian Keating.

Includes index.
ISBN 1-894856-50-3 (bound).—ISBN 1-894856-22-8 (pbk.)

    1. Animals—Juvenile literature.  I. Title.

QL49.K423 2004        590        C2004-902121-4

Fifth House Ltd.
*A Fitzhenry & Whiteside Company*
1511, 1800–4 St. SW
Calgary, Alberta T2S 2S5

1-800-387-9776
www.fitzhenry.ca

Free Teachers' Guide available

## ACKNOWLEDGMENTS

There are many people who have encouraged and inspired me in my work as a naturalist. First and foremost, I would like to thank my wife Dee for her encouragement, support, praise, and also for being my best critic. We met as workmates, became friends, and the rest is history. I would also like to thank my parents for buying me that first pair of second-hand binoculars when I was twelve and for helping me develop my interest in nature. I would also like to thank my grandpa, Colby Reesor, one of Alberta's first conservationists. When I was still a small boy on the prairie in Medicine Hat, he introduced me to the joy of being outside. Garth Thompson—my inspiration since 1982—thank you for being my guide in African exploration and for meeting me in places all over the world to do amazing adventures. Thank you to the countless guides and naturalists in parks around the world for showing me the wonder of their wildlife treasures. Bob Sandford, thank you for showing me that one can make a living as a naturalist and for being a true mentor during my college years. Ralph Westendorp, you gave me my first job in the field—thank you. Thanks, of course, to Peter Karsten, my equal in energy and enthusiasm, who hired me at the Calgary Zoo. And finally, thank you Bob Schadler, my childhood friend from New York, who was my partner in nature. Those endless hours in the woods, all those fossils and bird nests we gathered to create our own nature museum, it all helped me to become who I am today.

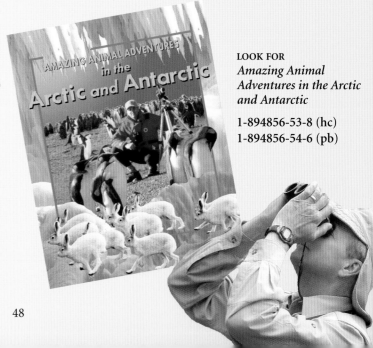

LOOK FOR
*Amazing Animal Adventures in the Arctic and Antarctic*

1-894856-53-8 (hc)
1-894856-54-6 (pb)